FREAKED

LIZ ROBBINS

ELIXIR PRESS
DENVER, COLORADO

 For information, address Elixir Press, PO Box 27029, Denver, CO 80227.

www.elixirpress.com

Author photo: Jenna Alexander
Cover art: Brianna Angelakis
Book design by Steven Seighman

Library of Congress Cataloging-in-Publication Data
Robbins, Liz (Elizabeth C.), 1971-
[Poems. Selections] Freaked / Liz Robbins.
pages ; cm
Includes bibliographical references.
ISBN 1-932418-55-5 (alk. paper)
I. Title.

PS3618.O315237A6 2015
811'.6—dc23 2014026884

10 9 8 7 6 5 4 3 2 1

". . . let us bless the freak; for in the natural evolution of things, the ape would perhaps never have become man had not a freak appeared in the family."

—Vladimir Nabokov

Contents

Acknowledgments

Many thanks to the editors of the publications in which these poems are forthcoming or first appeared, sometimes in different versions:

5 A.M.: "Man Chokes to Death on Pocket Bible"; *Baltimore Review*: "Heat"; *Barely South Review*: "A Kind of Cursing"; *Bone Bouquet*: "Gaffe Aftermath"; *Cimarron Review*: "Amy Visits Danica's Palm Reader" and "John and Amy's Song"; *Cold Mountain Review*: "Shadow Box"; *Cream City Review*: "[the virgin]"; *Gargoyle*: "Before the Cut"; *Hayden's Ferry Review*: "[the lion]"; *Iron Horse Literary Review*: "Class Reunion"; *The Journal*: "Sentences"; *Kenyon Review Online*: "[the crab]" and "[the ram]"; *Louisville Review*: "Rebellion as Ice Floe"; *Mezzo Cammin*: 'A Family on Their Lawn One Sunday in Westchester, NY, 1968' and "Mike's Rage"; *New Madrid*: "Winning Documentary"; *New York Quarterly*: "Warnings"; *Notre Dame Review*: "[the archer]" and "[the goat]"; *Permafrost*: "[the scorpion]"; *The Pinch*: "[the fishes]" and "genesis"; *Pisgah Review*: "Smoothie"; *Rattle*: "Drive-In Church"; *Southern California Review*: 'Identical Twins, Roselle, NJ, 1967' and 'A Young Man in Curlers at Home on West 20th Street NYC, 1966'; *Sugar House Review*: "Dry Spell"; *Sweet*: "Old Joke" and "Walk of Shame"; *Tar River Poetry*: "Doll with Purple Heart" and 'So Others May Live'; *Valparaiso Poetry Review*: "China Poem"; *Whiskey Island*: "Heartworks" (as "As My Sister Sews").

Much appreciation to Sonja Livingston, Tom Useted, and *The Pinch* crew for selecting "genesis" as a "Poem of the Month."

Much appreciation, too, to Edward Byrne and *Valparaiso Poetry Review* for selecting "China Poem" as a "Poem of the Week."

I am grateful to Gianna Russo, Sylvia Curbelo, and the YellowJacket Press team for selecting *Girls Turned Like Dials* (where some of these poems first appeared) for the 2012 YellowJacket Press chapbook prize.

My eternal thanks to Dana Curtis and Elixir Press. Post-solo clapping to Bruce Bond.

Dark rum barrels to Michael Waters. Rapid snowmelt to Frank X. Gaspar.

Thank you to my Flagler College colleagues and students.

And to DMR: *Ik hou van je.*

Introduction

Where there are freaks, there are families. There are circles of inclusion, lines to memorize, *t's* to cross, and the freak, as outsider, must be inside just enough to give voice to the something missing, new, or needed, something lost beyond acknowledgement of loss. Liz Robbins' bravely realized third book is just such a voice and yes, a little freakish, oddly shaped in places, rebellious yet self-questioning, funny-weird and funny-ha-ha, fierce and yet deftly reticent with its heartbreak, its authenticated rendering of what it is to feel both inside and outside the normative circle. Here we find a girl abandoned who, over time, cultivates abandon into first a lifestyle and then, by, secular grace, an art.

Where there are freaks, there are those who freak. It is the signature of a contemporary world, its fractured inheritance of values and myths, where *freak* becomes a verb and thus weds the anomaly to her distrust of others and, worse, of self. Chance too can feel like fate, the scattered stars as the authors of character, angelic orders that give us orders, but what we find in this book's opening sequence, "Star-Holder," is, like stars, both held and full of fire. Bitterness, dread, drunkenness and disappointment—they find acceptance in imagination's constellations, in the poem's yearning for connection and yet, as freaked, for an independent refuge. Thus we find the poem as conversation, as something that reaches out, acknowledges, challenges, recalls, however pitched at the speed of individual reverie. Where better to begin a book than with a thrill ride, and the age when it dawns on us that fear and desire are like that couple you knew in high school, at odds constantly, but fabled, fabulous, crazy in love.

In a world of impoverished choices where "everyone's pissed about his life station," these poems bear testament to imaginative abundance. While they have many of the grounding elements of narrative detail, they are never root-bound, never merely narrative, complacent with chronology. Abundance takes departure. It takes a freak. While we find in theme and method a dialogue between chaos and form here, it is the voice of the poems that gives them their expressive range: the wicked humor, the tenderness, the insight, the confusion. Voice—by turns self-ironic, dark, and compassionate—trumps form in a way that situates the poems in a fiercely personal, inward space, where the world appears as relational, as ever befriended, endured, kicked against. Metaphor too drenches these poems in subjectivity's euphoria and play, in spirits, if you will, like teenagers at a carnival. This is not to say the poems melt into the ether of their own devices. Figuration here is so brilliant because it is spot on, fresh and thereby attentive to self, other, and the place between, where poems refuse to extricate a world from why it matters.

The most radical form of rebellion, the kind with bite, the power to change us, the power to change itself, is precision. Finally, that is what surprises and gratifies me most about this book. Out of the wilderness, the candor, the funny kid in the grownup in the kid in the grownup, we find, in all its oddness and charm, wisdom. If freaks bless us in ways that allow for evolution, it may well be that they bring a new intelligence to the conversation. I know it is an illusion, but reading these poems, I feel part of that conversation—for while these poems are, in signature ways, unlike any others I have written or seen, I feel that they get me: the me I am, the me I have yet to become.

—Bruce Bond

1. STAR-HOLDER

[the virgin]

the scorpion, the rattler, the blue octopus—all the best
rides named for heart-stopping creatures, we were
thirteen and fear was bad or good, on the bus, jenn
and greg hid under a blanket and french kissed, we
were scandalized, envious—but the rattler had three
loops, the scorpion a body-lifting drop, all strung
about the smell of spun sugar sweat balloons, the
chaperones trudging to an old-timey picture stand
to dress like thieves and chiefs, posing for something
to bring back home—accepting rides was one thing
but those of us who went too many times didn't yet
sense the taste developing, the stomach-flip adult
somehow, gravity defied a moment—soaring above
a choppy sea of melted wax faces before plunging—
and yes we measured each other by it, as jenn and
greg strolled off wing in wing for soft serve, still
pink-cheeked, suspended for a time above us all

[the crab]

elaine, let me speak of the sign under which my folks were born,
the miraculous blue death we're sure to carry in our female parts
as we were chosen

to not use them intentionally—we may be emotional peasants but
not blind, no, not ruined—we grew more slowly, more fast than
girls who grew lush herb

gardens of people in their bodies, but we're all under one blue
umbrella with zig-zag clouds—a sign, as we have maybe three
hundred grand hours left—

our guts may shudder with human glass shards but the end disease
is not upon us yet, no, not that we know, not yet the tree upon which
the green moss feeds—

yet my mind still grows its red berries, some days sweet, some
deadly, this the lesson—

we built a hut with a thatched roof and the holes get us wet so
we take care now where we stand and patch—i may be misty but
i never shot a gun—

now if only everyone, all at once, kept on the safety—

if you light a candle for me, make sure it's red, don't forget, lick a
thumb and pointer—we're both holy and aflame, so before sleep
save yourself, douse the wick

[the archer]

what to say, amy, when the ambien's working
but only partially, you and john moved into
the apartment with a twenty-four hour door-
man, which is to say you're a sleepwalker
now asleep and awake, the 21st century shot
through the heart with sung chemicals like
when i go to the country and rest assured
across the river the factory will be open,
churning up condeleeza clouds and screwing
up wavelengths, no need to get me a sippy
cup, but i thought after all this time, your
father, and global bailouts, you could handle
revolving doors, what do you see, amy, when
you drift downstairs deformed at two a.m.,
i imagine the uniformed doorman a crayoned
barkeep ready to serve old ghosts, old hell-
bound troy who bought us a thousand shots
when we were underaged, for him we'd burn
an effigy, i'm all for marshals on planes but
i'm essentially a gypsy, dark-headed, plotting,
as all night stalkers who've lost their mooring

[the ram]

everyone's pissed about his life station, joel, me too, this job sucks
and it's the best thing that ever happened to us, imagine, real
redeemable checks to be

surrounded by the young, no it's not locked eyes on a disco floor
but neither is it a raft with finned horizons, more a box of kittens left
on the back porch we must

take in, feel the weight of the lead apron, the horns, the dank breath,
us to whom relationships are death and life, and here everyone
including us is lonesome

and toxic and sometimes not—i lose perspective, too, but then i'm in
the small-town diner, the only place in town, and the waitresses snarl
because their chicken is

perfect in its salt, it turns me into what woolf called vivienne, a string
of live weasels around eliot's neck—joel, your eyes haven't yet resigned
to patination, and if you

knock on my door, remember you're starting a ring of concentric
circles on what's essentially a square, meaning i may be playing statue
but for you sometimes i'll move

[the scorpion]

sooze, the radio jesus says our salvation must come
without body, i'm not willing to wait and you are,
the sax solo growing buttered layers as it complicates,
this explains all—

you a bee with pollination duty and me tree-sitting
with pretend lynchings—yes, the emotion opus cloud
both blue and violent in squalls, reflections of the lava
cough syrup on which

bobby means got drunk, since ninth grade the heart
batting lashes toward the most potential sting, every-
thing shaken over with black pepper—yes, a woman
must find her beauty

wheresoe're it lies, despite the old conscriptions, the
dried grape leaves in our beds, we designed to be each
other's hard reflection, one sister the nightingale's white
tape, the other bovary's

tired powders, when the ash and molten fire settle down,
i'll be handcuffed, you buoyed, but both blinking girlish
dreams, tweaking overgrown thickets, the resurrected
berries laughing

[the lion]

so we had no choice but to attend
danica and mike's divorce party where
the banner reads BFF but somewhere
an owl goes, who cooks for you, who
cooks for you all, the gifts we brought
the same as when they married but now
in twos, stuffed on the makeshift ark
bar, mike with his golden mane and
beard a kind of god still controlling—
a lightweight boxer in tribal mask—and
danica as ever his beauty and the beast
bell, handing out like a secretary leaflets
on doorprizes, of course, lottery ticket
scratch-offs, oh america where you
lose money but the entertainment of
doing so is free, later when we're drunk
we'll do the rumba on the deck of the
titantic and later still hold a seance for
ice floes in the north pacific slicked
with oil, yes, every one of us complicit
in the shortage of smack, mobbing for
scrapple, lying horizontal in wrecked
flower beds, this the visceral, as we
heed the siren call on the premise
the threads have finally ripped, no,
a divorce party not a crisis of heat
after all, but a kind of leprosy, you
get out the vacuum in the morning
to clear the shed skin from sheets

[the goat]

don, when you're gone, i go over
one-eighty, smoke marlboros, snort
sliders, rock to the eagles at two a.m.,
which is to say you rein me in from
the dystopic, yes i'm sadly narcissistic,
fresh from the placenta with elvis
dreams, the whitest powders for my
skis, if i inhale, will you hold safe
my diaphragm, we're in a bad fellini
film with liquidated feelings and red-
button-coated goats named cheney,
but we haven't moved yet to stripping
malls, aka, selling black market game-
boys—we're laying down backyard
pavers and for me it's like at five, those
years dad fled to albany, everywhere clear
abandonment, and as usual, i fly down
country backroads with the windows
open a green day song wirecutting
the fence, felling the song of all those
living trees—so yes, i buy the green
chinese kimono identity, don, and my
seabird tweets are getting you down
as you're all majestic egret, but let's
hope the boat on the river forgot its
binocs because we're shorebound for
now and i'm sliding down the zipper

[the scales]

we bought a plot of land in the country with the idea we'd build on it when we got old but the farmer neighbors got tired of looking at all that flat mere promise and suddenly there were rows and tiny white flowers all over and beneath the soil rooted tubers and we said *hey, that's our land* and they said *we'll give you a couple hundred to dig up your potatoes* and from then on we counted differently what with those new eyes

[the fishes]

kim, i sing a song to the girl you adopted
in beijing, to your gun-show arms from
holding firm, related, years ago the cow
and pig on your plate going the way of
dodo birds, forgive me for the song, eel
sleeking from privacy's underwater caves,
i too the goldfish blinking stunned in the
won clear bag, otis redding goes *i been
loving you too long* as we ride the El to
the art institute where the wide-eyed oils
have been somewhat quarantined, and
we're blown away, wind plashing us
upward—kim, when i go walking in dark
complexes i think i may disappear, to be
a woman holds this fear, and we are in-
mates set free to pave a road in tar, where
to pick up the plot—in other words, keep
getting me to straighten up, salt the skin,
pull the gentlest fruit from trees, our words
tumbling soon to denouement, but you're
already sold, more free in your girl's arms
than a sworn lord transmogrified to wine

[the water-bearer]

sara, used to be i let the sun directly on
my face, i'm turning old, the lure of
Impressionistic art in cities i've begun
to turn from, no lie, i pulled up the truck
and saw a dead wild turkey bottle
and knew I was saved by which i mean
i may at anytime break from my body
into flotsam, oh i know, but i only crib
the best, ain't no wright, but there's this
artist type, a poet, so in love with new
love she whores the writer's circuit and
has babies in between, i kinda get
addictions to life's-not-fair endings,
which is why the merchandise is hot
and i always burn my tongue—listen,
manatees swim past in a ballet of boat-
scarred skin and our exposure to this
world is death, the rows of cabbage
heads, brown leaves reeking soft earth,
sulphur—i may be silly to keep falling,
but it's not so bad to hope to go Up
North for the last round, corpse going to
ground unburned, yes it's a kind of selfish
gift to pour all over everyone but it does
some good, the rain

[the twins]

laura, if i had to define my particular badness, it's that i invite
too many days to begin with the tiny pity violin, immune to
recalling the won horseshoe games—

today it rains and instead of dragging around the apartment
with cigarettes, let's bust out the songbook of sea chanties!
your side of the room looks like a hotel and mine Beirut,
which is why you're such a good

writer—in the movie of our life, the camera would zoom in
on your white throat, hands massaging in the white cream
meanwhile, i'm in the kitchen with a sticky frying pan, crepes
burned and raw—

later we'll go to the student colloquium and you'll hear things
and use them and i'll hear things and take them personally—
me and julio down by the schoolyard hums you

and mine's no more a faux life than yours, it's just you actually
get to the gym, your slept-with list thinner than mine—

you go out in the day and i stay in, the apartment becomes
a shotgun shack teeming with bad-dream melting clocks
and skyscraper mice—

but the cellphone is a vine from your ear to mine and when
you tell me your poem just died, little pink sorrow buds pop
up and this is how we are

friends, i may sing *a case of you* as i get clean, but nothing
is gone till forgotten—when you get home we'll uncork chablis,
the remember-when stories, choose the smoother stones
to pile as we mark our loved and buried

[the bull]

beverly, i'm by the marina, sitting down in a public bathroom
stall, and this woman says to her friend, *remember? i was*
looking for a sign? well this hand dryer i just noticed says
bradley crossing so now i feel happy and certain, and this
is what i mean when i say elephants and planets and bills
don't fit on a flag, it's wonky perspective, and we're in the
blazing-hot weeds, superstitions like daisies, cheery as they
poison the real flowers—oh, don't be a snob, but i know you
agree and neither blew ourselves up, stark raving mad, i'm
not going to fake it anymore—bev, as my country friend
says, it's time to talk chickens, it's time for the donkeys to
come home to boost, we may be sore afraid, the song
shrill, but the rules got all bent, all split-infinite and punny
and it's past time to point to the dark cloaks and guns that
get us grounded, the fattest one a bound book and alas
i see it burning but what goes first, us or the market?

11. LINE-TRACKER

Drive-In Church

My mother wakes early every Sunday, pulls on black
hose even in June, and drives forty minutes to put on
a choir robe and sing in a crowd for a crowd. Such is
the nature of her faith. Mine was held for too many
years thrashing under water, burbling, silent-screaming
for air. My faith may be, however, growing toward that
church in Daytona Beach, where you don't even have to
get out your car and therefore your pajamas, just tool
right up with your ciggy's on the dash and a 12-pack
of Krispy Kremes, reggae on the tape deck. Where you
can snooze mid-sermon, curl up with a blanket and
nobody'd see. With only your license plate showing,
you'd still get credit for going. That's what I mean, it's all
about the redeemer card for me, where 999 church visits
means a trip to heaven is free. My mother says, *It's not
for God you go, for you.* But I'm still that teen in black
eyeliner and dress, scowling in the back pew, stinking
of last night's beer, wondering what's in it for me. Which
doesn't add up, if my mother's to be believed. Here's what
I think. One day I'll die and maybe it'll be true, my mother
wearing wings, drinking martinis, laughing in the golden
sun beyond a big locked gate, and I'll be staring in, feeling
sorry and alone, yet knowing I'm exactly where I'm meant
to be. And my mother says, *How is that unlike now and
how you've felt your whole life? Maybe if you'd go to
church, you'd feel different.* And I say, Doesn't someone
have to be the crazy, the heathen? What if everyone went
to church? She sighs, *oh if I know God, He'd just find
another way to up the ante.* To which I think, the next
time I go looking in the paper for drive-in times, it'll be
to see what film's playing. But she knows I'm listening.

"So Others May Live"

—Four members of a Buffalo, New York, junior firefighters club admitted to setting twelve fires and reporting thousands of false alarms over a three-year period because they wanted to aid firefighters who complained of boredom.

When Miss Clark read us that poem about the fire
truck in the rain, the *wheels rumbling / through*
the dark city, it turned my mind, I heard if not harps,
then my mom ringing the supper bell. I knew I'd join,
I'm the leader, the others follow, though it's not what
you think, black trenchcoated, graffiti-spraying teens
bent on mayhem. Picture three guys and a girl trying
on turnout gear, dreams aflame in red and black,
Michigan Street Baptist Church smoking like a room
in hell, or all of Millionaire's Row lit up in hot gold.
The point is, it's only fun once, sliding down the pole,
only so many ways to make chili. The cable TV with
no Xbox, and the public service flyers never needing
updates, ie. Christmas Tree Safety, *never use lit candles*
to decorate a tree. We're old enough now to find the
brown spot on Ernie's face growing black and Mike's
Zoloft in the fridge, and when you walk in the station
and so many are taking naps, it makes you want to clang
and howl, drag them all into the day's onrush. We're
young enough still to not lose much, the thousand-hour
volunteer mark getting you a hoodie with a patch, not
a guaranteed career, so why not blow it on them while
the kid fantasy's still alive, tearing down streets, siren
screaming, Hummers and Mercedes bowing down?
There's no moving backward once you get going, and
the first thing they taught us was the firefighter's motto.

A Kind of Cursing

—Senator Matthew Feldman introduced a bill into the New Jersey Senate to allow a $1,000 fine and six months in jail for anyone who profits by guaranteeing a "curse" on a person's enemy through use of, for example, the "evil eye," demons, voodoo, "bones," or pronouncing magic words of the occult designed to bring bad luck.

I live in Daytona Beach, land of contradictions. Students strip to sunbathe on Spring Break outside condos where the snow-haired keep vigil on pulses. If I lived in Hoboken, I wouldn't fear fines: necessary work I do, knowledge of bodies. I am a factory of one, molding little red dolls from warm wax that hardens smooth. The contract in triplicate: one for you, one for me, a third for the doll who acts as third party—a kind of father, son, and ghost, though what I do does not kill, a clean trick one can't outrun by car, plane, or prayer. The pin slides in the shoulder, bursitis. The genitals, a virus. The heart, and she is friendless. At midnight, doll in hand, I sip pinot noir, wait for the right pain to suggest itself, spot-lit. A vibe, an invented song. My pulse jackrabbits to the moon floating above the Atlantic. Froth on ocean waves means change. Crying brings solace, relief. I give third parties simple bad luck, as from bad luck eventually comes good. Pain helps revise themselves for better. Each doll costs an even grand. And I do not claim to cure you who makes the order.

Man Chokes to Death on Pocket Bible

—The medical examiner speculated that the 22-year-old Franco Bruno had tried to swallow the 874-page Bible to purge himself of the Devil.

Labyrinths in the prehistoric ages served as traps
for evil spirits, but I adore it here in Franco's body.
The entrance is birth and the exit God but so many
turns to get lost in, to plant vices. For months now,
I've explored his brain's gray maze, turned flowering
girls to mean drunks and parents to shrieking crows.
I murdered the monk, sewed his nose and lips shut,
said a few sincere curses over flopping limbs. Days
after, he crawled with silver flies. It's not my fault,
how I tick. The body in all its lushness my sphere,
how easily it darkens to overripe. My sole gripe:
thoughts of children I must doom to candy green
apples poison-dipped, tiny bones of fish lodged in
tiny throats. I must admit a chill when I see thoughts
like a red poppy field running spring-crazed and
laughing. Reminds me of the finished and hopeful
words of a priest's blessing and then I could almost
gouge out my eyes, stick bamboo beneath my nails
in penitence, start edging my way to the holy center.
But it'd be wrong to go against nature, so I place in
Franco a thought of what to do instead with divine
words on pages. Soon, I'll be crawling out like a fly,
soon, entering the ear of another good man, confused.

Doll with Purple Heart

—The Hasbro toy company withdrew its decision to market its "Zartan the Enemy" soldier doll as a "paranoid schizophrenic" that gets violent. Several mental health organizations had complained the marketing was in poor taste and misrepresentative of mental illnesses. A Hasbro vice president apologized.

Why the hysteria? We'd also planned a companion
good soldier doll who salutes and holds a gun that
pops and smokes. You yank the string in his back
to hear him say, *God bless the U.S.A.* and *Dulce et*
decorum est. A tribute to my uncle Ned, once up to
his kneecaps in rice paddies. All the dolls today are
girls like Barbie, impossible heroes like Superman.
What of the dark interior, the crashing boredom and
jittered belly, the blinking up at strange tree canopies?
Even today he dreams in Vietnam jungle pageantry,
the rat-a-tat near and far, his speech a.m. radio static,
chatter of snowmen brigades finally splitting the yoke
from the white. He's like a father, and if I could, I'd
add a beer for the cracked throat, a rag for the head
dotted with fever. A hooded poncho to keep features
from blurring in warm rain.

Rebellion as Ice Floe

—Three teenage boys in NYC stole a woman's purse and tried to make their getaway by jumping onto a five-by-four-foot slab of ice floating down the Hudson River. They were stranded on the ice until rescued by police helicopter.

Who among us cannot recall those years of barking dogs
that only disobedience would silence, when risk immersion
was a kind of tomato-soup-and-toasted-cheese-sandwich
waiting beyond the blind blizzard of hormones and parental
shoulds? A black pill in a bottle reading *may contain cyanide*
swallowed whole and thoughtlessly. My parents tried.
Church every weekend, Sunday School, the lasting lesson
of the prodigal son (no matter what you do, you will be loved,
you will be saved) becoming fact, becoming daughter.
Something warm and staggered about the hunger that helped
me lift the window screen, inch my body across the roof,
stretch into the maple's limbs, shimmy down, and hustle
through the dark to my father's car, cold in the driveway.
Even the planning before, an ecstacy: what waited beyond
the yard's split-rail fences? Starting the car, the taste of warm
beer and strange boys' tongues. Release's erasure. How alone
I was and fearless, sinking in deep autonomy's needle. How
little I knew, stuck in the reach-out-and-grab delirium, assuming
a hard run would bring safety, not paralysis. Like when I backed
down our driveway's hill, only to stall at the bottom. Trying to
turn an engine that never caught, then heaving my full weight
against the back of the car, trying to push it back up. Finally
red-faced, having to shake awake my father. His anger expected,
but not his sigh of acceptance and later, his laughter. The true
lesson of the prodigal dawning years after, what only the lucky
get, seeing clear as for the first time so many good parents and
kids around, and how it's still a choice to save even our own.

Brazilian Cannibal Sect Makes Human-Filled Empanadas

The voice commands we do away with evil women.
We intuit the wicked, and then it is slicing the tough outer layers
of mangoes. They do not come back as ghosts. We are three,
man wife mistress, we have little money. We are singing mouths,
tongue machetes. Freezer hum, the half moon cycling. The feeding
of insects, a state of becoming, a monastery, and the stain is
raw beets. The women, spiny
jackfruit. Blood lights the tips of ancestral spears. Behind funeral
pyres, the painted faces of saints. A good fire quelling need.
Solitude suggesting madness, and *we dine on the flesh of evil*
as a purification ritual. We bury the remainder in the patio.
We sew them in dough, fry in oil, sell. And you eat. And strive
to purge dark from this good world as we do, knowing and not,
and we call you monkey heart.

Because the Sweet Cherry Algebra of Door Locks

—A house burglar in Logan, Oregon, known as "The Muncher," has broken into rural homes to eat food, drink beer, watch TV, and then clean up after himself.

Because the rifle is rusted, or no one will fire it.

Because defeat means whiskey-ed and sleepless in motels.

Because of the many detective shows that deal with forensics.

Because the white bowl in the fridge bleeds tart strawberries.

Because the gems in dark blue boxes are usually rhinestones.

Because the override of the mind's urgent arguments.

Because above the front door flies an arrogant striped flag.

Because with gingersnap cookies wolves shapeshift to puppies.

Because a gesture of domination doesn't have to be violent.

Because a boat in a storm and days of jagged rocks.

Because every porch light could be a beacon.

Because the bed's clean white sheets will remain.

Because threat of danger is a flutter above the rib cage.

Because the thrill of fishing is the lake's black water.

Because violation is an unforgettable catch in the throat.

Two Soviet Inventors Request a Patent in 1986 for an Edible Vodka Bottle That, When Digested, Reduces Blood Alcohol Level

We designed this for you, by which we mean
all of us who desire waking up on beds or streets. We
may or may not hide our personal gods in a sack. A kind
of rigor, a commitment, to drink from the perfect
clear bottle pulled from perdition's dry ice. Highball glasses
mist beside the handrolled cigarettes. Beyond the sheeted furniture
of childhood's home, the journey post-adults. You who break
padlocks return between the aesthetics of freedom
and grief. Hours, ghosting the crushed ice, orbiting the cut-
grass summer smell, the pine-needled winters--ricochet of
insides you keep trying to disinfect. An improbable feat:
to dislodge from your throat the still-alive hope song,
and when you disembark once again from the blessèd
dying motorboat, you'll need something to eat.

Sacred Cat Rug

—for an ex

You always loved cats more than dogs or people, so tonight I've broken into the Villa Zorayda and stolen the Sacred Cat Rug just for you. The rug is cursed. At 2400 years, it's the oldest in the world. Older than certain prayers of devotion. It was found in the river Nile by a man who likes to fish. It was found in the casket of a mummified princess, her foot broken off by graverobbers, stripped of its toe rings and anklets. Scientists have proven the spellbinding effects of young beauty and gold. Scientists have proven the rug woven from hairs of worshipped live cats, light strands like those of certain young women. The curse: death to anyone who walks on it. In the '70's, a twenty-two-year-old rebel visiting the museum touched his foot to the rug and died a year later. In the '90's, the rug was removed to be cleaned, and the next day, a dead cat found on the steps. With this rug, I thee leave, too, the mummified foot, this incomplete summary. Because

I don't wish you dead
but to think of me onward
stepping carefully

Palm Reading

Accept your past as dirty snow.

You cannot come late to what he'll reveal, as to your own death.

The room is pumpkin incense, purple amulets.

You are at the water's edge. Drink.

He studies your hand, tours the hundred rooms, each with a sink.

His body shines the yellow aura of charlatan and saint.

The entire town, silent with listening.

When he speaks, the wind of your mind empties.

He builds an empty stadium with the sound of two palms clapping.

He tells a truth horribly serious and funny, a cartoon anvil dropping.

He draws the map to underground prisons, buried wells.

Accept the present, a plot of worms and wild mint.

What he reveals will be less stark prophecy, more calico prayer.

His eyes roll over the drive-in screen of blue movies.

Accept the future, a field of brown flowers.

To take home, a jar of live crickets to feed or pass on.

III. HEART-READER

Danica Visits a Palm Reader

Like martyrdom, the red-handed white sign.
Inside the house, college radio reggae,
rhythm threaded with rose incense, stray
women. Door opens. Dyed-black bob, wine
lips. *Come in.* Smell of holy lilies dead in brine.
I'm Jan. Tarot stack on a skull and bones tray.
She shuffles, wide-spreads, stares, blinks, starts to say,
stops. Then, *I look in your eyes, you into mine.*
Jan's blue irises reflecting in snow.
Your aura's green, you require much healing.
You've been wounded, or you anticipate
a wound. Green stands for nature. But Danica knows
her Death card means envy: so long, she's been kneeling
before the ax. Mike's rage, warming the plate.

Mike's Rage

Past porches, the night's parched wind unfurls,
peels layers from the spindle legs of girls.
Danica's out with Amy, Jill, and Jess.
The downtown spotlight spins in white distress.

I walk to Gyp's, the brown-lit, paneless bar,
her moon face smears in every passing car.
Lights clench and whistles tear. I order shots,
and build the inner fire of sticks and knots.

Soon I'll hear the wheat field, darkened farm
where once I hid. Blue corners tight with arms
and leather, flinches.
                                                  When hours grow young,
I'll see her blank thighs soundlessly unstrung.
Smell the wind's blood-knuckled fists and dirt.

The girls go by, scissoring in skirts.

Amy Visits Danica's Palm Reader

and it's a dream she couldn't have imagined:
the one-story house devoid of color.
Jan in a beige dress. Tan carpet. White doors.
Jan, stoic, but of Mediterranean
descent, and everywhere, angels: one pinned
to Jan's chest. Ten plaster statues on the floor,
eight figurines by the Tarot cards. Eight more
on posters: all white and gold. Has Amy sinned?
Is she a bad girlfriend needing forgiveness?
Sure enough: *I see blockage. Fear. Black clouds.*
Tell me about your love relationship . . .
and Amy's drunk at Friday's in a red dress.
John slams a shot, bored. Stands, slips into the crowd,
and there's blood. Silent Amy, biting her lip.

Amy Gives Blood

The Blood Mobile may save lives,
but John cannot be cajoled
to enter. The needles like knives.
Red rubber ball, a world to hold

and release. Amy's light head clears.
Outside, she flaps her arm gauze:
Add blood to your list of fears
and phobias! John blinks, jaw

tightening. The hot thick bags like cuts
of beef, they couldn't save his dad.
Lung cancer. An urn filled with butts.
What oppressive hours he'd had,

coughing up lakes of black fire,
hospital sheets wet with regrets.
John, unable to grant desires:
More hours. A pack of cigarettes.

John and Amy's Song

John breaks up with Amy, and she implodes--
raw insides, red, bleating. All her heart's roads
leading to a nunnery in Brazil,
The Church of Christ's Spit at the top of a hill
she can't quite climb, steep with red ants, nude trees.
But no John? How will she fill her need to please?
Her rubbing-John's-feet, her making-beef-stew?
Belief in herself a well-known hymn, all dew
and daisy smell, averted gaze and bow.
John knows his role, too; see how gently now
he folds Amy in arms, slings the break, her
sadness, his . . . . she, the lone parishioner
speaking in tongues, soaking the funeral pyre
at the Mountain of Miracles and Fire.

Danica Explains Her Enemy

His wife, I've heard, is *unstable.*
His wife, he tells me, cranks James Brown,
and with a cleaver makes too-shallow grooves
in the kitchen table. She does not feel good,
screams at him in showers. Liquid raging
down on his head as she appears ghostly
beyond the curtain: *You left on the fucking*
kettle!, as he explains, *I meant to, I want*
tea when I get out. Still he takes it out on
me, his co-worker at the elementary school,
and for this, he is more adversary than
friend. Fires off emails: *Can you cover*
my class this morning? We're on chapter twelve
in Science, the different forms water can take.
Little curls like steam rise from the Arial
font and he'll be angry if I refuse and
angry if I accept, my life benign enough
to unclench the fist, let in his sweet-eyed
students. What he cannot know: the thorny
lines on my thighs, dug there by a razor
replaced after five times, cuts swabbed by
gauze dunked in alcohol. What I cannot
accept: seeking out pain is a brand of
indulgence. That by the laws of every known
species of rose, my enemy's suffering is more
precise, less tinged with precious pink,
than my own. I know, but don't accept.
Which is why I hear the train whistle blow in
the red hours of morning. Why I can only go
sometimes inside the warm circle of children.

IV. FEAR-BEARER

Genesis

so to the task, pseudo-adam, rattler-in-an-adam-
mask, adam-fallen-short, of calling things by
their longing names, the schlitz cans holding
love-that-is-not-love potion, party where we met
a hot-body constellation, yours apple-scented,
under-shirted--already the twisted-about-the-neck
cord growing, the nearly-bored code of silence,
our across-the-room eyes a kind of radiation--
this the prologue to our fortune-cookie opera,
the mystifying *fog of today conceals the dark-*
ness of your future, yes, there you are at two
a.m. amtraking the porch, one last stop for
un-ticketed girls, and i outside-but-soon-to-
be-in your fled-eden diorama, dazzled, yes,
imagined doves flitting stone-castle eaves,
he restoreth my soul, the snow-dress-with-
train lie already weaving like eggs in a sac--
only after years could i track the taste to skim,
your milky skin, control at whim the proud
battery revving mind and body, we after all
not the distance, but a black-swan flurry of
wings, a dazing tunnel cloud soon to finish
off the already-trashed prairie

Sentences

—after Nicanor Parra

God is a bigfoot. Giant squid of the deep.
The last seaside resort. A Mexican standoff.

No joke. The airplane stays aloft by collective
wishing. Art is a rich and gray soil. Money, green

shoots in a field of dead clover. Dogs are Buddha,
are rooting, court jesters. Ice cream is fashion, is

prayer books. God is a wig, a wink, a coat of wool.
Ecstasy, a burp, a remodeled interior, an accident

of two. Or faith. Babies, patchwork quilts, the bed
itself. Bicycles, fringe. The heartland, suede.

Darkness, a president. A party. A beacon. God is
a script. In pencil. Traced over in red ink.

Warnings

—after Nicanor Parra

No wedding nights allowed. No after-hours lighting.

No intentional darkening. No necking, no wetting, no spreading. No splitting or joining, no expelling. No toe-curling. No moaning, no relieving. No smoking, no walking on grass.

No adoptions permitted. No unearthing, no birthing. No products made of metal. No mentoring, no exampling. No birding, no catting. No dogging, no babying. All holds barred.

No windows left open. Outside airs forbidden. No churning, no burning, no blacking out. No striking, no signing, no brainstorming. No knobbing on doors. No bread scarfing, no wining.

No clocks or clock-making.

In this district, absolutely no making, period. No making up or out, or beds in which one lies. No fringes or firings. No leavings. No greenings. No whispering in phones.

No forsaking, no fishing. No zones. No dangling from wires.

Wedding Night

My loneliness had grown so acute like a fresh green tomato turned
ordinary red despite its intentions.

You, enough like me, a bowl of dark cherries.

After the ceremony, we sat on the hotel roof, sipping Cabernet, looking
for stars winking in the sky. What could be prophecy, proof.

We blew through matches. Strike-light-strike again. Burning through
the wine's paper sack.

Something had gone true.

I didn't wait to remove catacombs, my long lace dress. We were alone
in a star-boat that rocked like a cradle. A plugged tub

but with the sea outside. We turned in to one another.

I didn't want a third, to be a mother. I, a happy betrayer. The bassinet
wheeled in with a monkey, or onion, or bomb.

This is how I knew you were mine, you saying we didn't have to.

We undressed and our bodies pulsed red in the dark for whole minutes
without moving.

Together, we were almost good, blood-relationed. Blessed. Or ordinary
in the old and new helix.

Winning Documentary

We were a four-person camera crew in Afghanistan, where the story was still about getting the Afghans to form their own army.

The real story was getting them to take us seriously.

The real story was getting

a story about anything but ourselves. Even though it was a story about us, we pretended it was not about us winning. It was

the 2020's.

Memoir had become too garish. Too much

a wager on hoarded relationships. People were scarce. Technology, a private and pervasive nerve agent.

Yes, there was the requisite

moon, a nod to sentimentality, but we weren't allowed to film the men showering, where they washed away

the dirt. Left the red imprints of guns.

They yawned through target practice. There was little we could use.

The dream was a gallery in Soho, our film on stately screens. Here, the snow of inaccessible TV. We'd imagined ourselves circling

a desert bonfire at night, where ideas like embers would sift from philanthropic

auras. Instead, the men stole

opium and bullets to sell to the Taliban, stuck them in open lockers. They knew there were no rules, not yet. No god

figure censoring. No jailer. Just the men, who'd begun dodging

showers. We recognized this as a refusal of the call, which ticked us off. Whose journey was this? Their black hair slicked

with sweat as they stood in a row, pins on a card.

We could hardly shoot them.

One of them asked us to explain the word *lunacy*.

And we had thought we'd drift in the night desert as in a cool inlet. We'd thought Afghanistan a dark easy river pricked with diamonds.

Our lens, the sieve we'd pull them through.

Dry Spell

To visit, I wear the Goodwill jade green silk
with the knot at the throat. All winter we were hot
with envy. You open the door, red-eyed. Hunger
makes you cry. You've been barefoot with the new
baby in your heart, standing in your too-clean office,
eating the darkness. Your work, scattered, and I, alone
with no baby. *Men kick friendship around like a football,*
but it doesn't seem to crack. You hand me a glass of
bitter iced tea, made sweet with coconut milk, and lead
me to the nursery, where an antique doll sits, one eye
slit. What aphrodisiac for friendship? I've chased you
hard for months, wanting back the dark soil we pushed
from to equal height. Now one's too high. One of us,
cheated. Nothing levels like fire, a domestic ritual.
My ice cubes clink. *Women treat friendship like glass,*
and it goes to pieces. Do I need new spectacles?
I'm working through the reasons. No spells exist
to make a friend stay. So I dream a hoodoo fusion
pyre: yellow roses, pear blossoms, a photo of Japan's
dolphin slaughter. Wave the smoke up and away.

Shadow Box

We fly north in snow to bury your father. Tall windows of the country
house, the lake a hard fogged mirror. I understand parts when you speak.
Alone we process negatives: bed pan, stale air, mouth ajar. New the dark
irreversibles. Flash of dandelion heads in grass, plastic chairs in shallows.
Early summer light close, Dutch-Mastered. But this the usual ragged circle.
No blood sacrifice. No tongue or hands cut free to keep secrets. Even the
snow not unwhite. But some of us need rage. Talk turns to god, governance,
money. The many scales. Near, the fish slowed beneath ice. Hard to expose.
I run the lake, exhaling him, cold twinge above hips. Winter more near.
The trees unmoved, I love you. To the new black dress, I'll pin a gold leaf.

Gaffe Aftermath

Rain dispels the pollen
gossip. Tension tendrils.
I am really so monstrous.
Not newborn, but invisible
spinster vindictive. Horrifying
in her attention bonfire.
Benders can't free the already
terror drunk! Sepia stain
befalls the white cloth, and
escape in sleeping doesn't
come. Space unwide enough.
Noplace is crouch, soothe.
The overturned stew tureen!
Half-circle friends erode.
Flip a penny, give or cry.
The problem's always been.
What needle more potent?
Too much give. Bad
attention turns weeping.

Class Reunion

To prepare, I crack the memory
vault, thick with road dust. There
still, the green king and queen
of Homecoming. High school
was a ruination by fire, spiraling
me soot-black and coughing
toward a truer self. Too tempting
to call high school a noose, a smile
in desperation. More like pinball:
the bang-skitter from clique to
clique. Only the stars knowing
the real gold lay in joining after-
school clubs. Some of us, knitting
together in fright, some turning
nomadic. All leaving to be Mason
jars in Tennessee. Destined to
pollute, roll, perhaps break. But I
have yet to get there. Back-pedaling
my old bike outside the gym,
afraid. The neighborhood's tiny
houses lit from within. Oh, to
have earned the wise man's
beard. To be well-heeled, or first.
Some good person's martyr.
Instead, my pedaling exhausts.
All my change, my thought, into
this gold lamé purse.

V. SOUL-STILLER

"A Young Brooklyn Family Going for a Sunday Outing, NYC, 1966"

A housewife with fat arms and beehive hair
holds props to hide herself from the quick-eyed
world: lace-haloed baby, leopard coat, pair
of binoculars for clarity. They lied:
friends, grandmother, mother, sisters, aunts.
Thick eyeliner and slutty coat, the last stab.
Her husband, black leather jacketed, wants
Xmas-morning joy for them, to catch a cab
to Mars. Grips his four-year-old son's hand
who's itchy in a wool sweater, face berserk
from standing still. The kid understands
the baby's his mother's joy and work:
she holds it high out of reach, a favorite toy.
He is what his father was, a wild-eyed boy.

"A Family on Their Lawn One Sunday in Westchester, NY, 1968"

Just what his father was, a wild-eyed kid,
is difficult to envision now (Dad covers
his eyes, tired from the sun, Mom's in the mid-
life crisis bikini.) Their son discreetly hovers
above a blue inflated pool in the yard,
leans down to gaze at his own small face.
His parents, lying long in chairs, are guards:
their bodies turned away to smaller traces
of comfort: stuffed ashtray, the full glass
on the table in between. Their weekend bliss:
the country club tan. Their weekend pass:
him running the yard. They do not kiss
or touch, but once they did. Dad eyeing Mom's hips,
some years before the boy's name crossed their lips.

"A Jewish Giant at Home With His Parents in the Bronx, NY, 1970"

Back before the boy's name crossed her lips,
Eddie's ambitious mother dreamed her son
a great man: a hero on horseback with whips,
movie contracts, straight spine, blond wife, fake guns.
A great man he became, eight feet high.
Played in movies, too: son of Frankenstein's
monster. Looking at him, Father thinks, *Why*
me. Mother thinks, *A nightmare, but he's mine.*
Eddie looks down on them, leans on a cane
(back hunched, shoes thick-soled), dying of bone disease.
The silent agreement: they don't complain
aloud, he pays the rent, aims to please:
TALLEST COWBOY AT RINGLING BROTHERS'!
A lifelong dream fulfilled (his mother's).

"Boy With Straw Hat Waiting to March in a Pro-War Parade, NYC, 1967"

A lifelong dream fulfilled (his mother's):
that he'd be loyal, patriotic, strong,
have his own opinions. He wears his brother's
old bow tie and suit. He can't be wrong,
to SUPPORT OUR BOYS IN VIETNAM
(button on his vest, which also reads God Bless
America. Another button reads BOMB
HANOI), especially since it's anyone's guess
whether or not his brother's still alive—
flat on his belly, elbowing through wet
rice paddy fields—and who just might arrive
home in time for Xmas, a displaced vet.
For now, the boy grips a new flag in his hand,
posed, as if someone showed him where to stand.

"Identical Twins, Roselle, NJ, 1967"

Posed, as if someone showed them where to stand,
the identical twin girls are close enough,
touching arms: lace tights, black frocks, white cloth bands
like gauze around their heads. This is the stuff
of twins: names that rhyme, everything the same,
including DNA. An accident,
the egg split. And now the Humpty-Dumpty game:
to get them back to the original intent:
a singular confection. The smiling twin
on the right, she's already sweetened fast.
The twin on the left frowns, sour. She won't win,
she'd rather be different, stung. She'll be passed
over for jobs, boyfriends. Soon, they'll both know it:
One will be the beauty. One, maybe the poet.

"Young Couple on a Bench in Washington Square Park, NYC, 1965"

One of them's a beauty. One, a poet.
She's thin, dark, doe-eyed—her bones, a spare frame
for him, a work of art: he's tight-jeaned, stoic—
shirt, undone. Face, a god's. You can't blame
him for sitting spreadeagled (one leg snaps
hers down). He's conquered New York, faces
the crowd, all the city bowing to his lap.
She's doomed to love those who take up spaces,
to coo her tributes softly, as she knows
withdrawal's imminent. She writes, *His eyes*
are lit windows in a field of night snow.
But it's not right. For Halloween, he'll tie
laurel leaves, a toga. She'll be a French maid, or
whore. Kneel by the bed in heels he paid for.

"A Young Man in Curlers at Home on West 20th Street, NYC, 1966"

Kneeling gingerly in heels he paid for
dancing in burlesque shows for wealthy men,
the transvestite looks under the bed he made for
Diane's sake, rummages, turns sullen when
he can't find his Jackie O knockoff pearls
(an homage to Diane's former life
as heir to Russeks Furs on Fifth Ave—the girl
who married at eighteen, became a housewife,
now divorced). He straightens, lights a cigarette,
stares past the lens to Diane, who kneels
behind it sans jewelry, in foul clothes, cool sweat.
She asks questions, tries to freeze what he feels.
What he'd most like to be (if some rich man cared)?
A housewife with real pearls and beehive hair.

VI. MIND-GAZER

Before the Cut

Ah, Central Park in spring. What a good day
for you to grow a mustache, me to grow
up! All around, last month's dead grass.
Let's set our blanket here for the noonday
sprawl. Have I told you about my kid-
napping fantasy? It ends with me gagged
and bound in a church, with my rescuer
leaping through a pane of stained glass.
Each color, reflecting a shade of
cowardice. Perhaps after we kiss
you could try some police helicopter
noises. But how to relax when the sky
is tepid tea? The crinkle around your
eyes, the sound of your cigarette pack.
You look so trendy in those smog-
dyed jeans, especially when you're
smoking! How long have we been dating?
How long till the starter dog? My uterus
is a pass/fail test. Earthenware jug dried
of wine, and your neck smells familiar,
like incense and something. In a minute,
I'll go with my nail scissors to cut you
a spray of green and gold weeds. I'm just
waiting for the sound of blades, slicing the sky.

Walk of Shame

A bit of a misnomer, as if the shame
were hers. As if it were not I
but her mother, father, brother, her more
chaste friends peeping out the window.
Their shame coarsens her
veins, blooms her face. Curly hair, thick
thighs, too-short blue dress, stepping from
the black Corvette with dark windows
and ragtop in morning. An older man,
and her head is down, small smile played
about her lips, feet bare. Hips swing as she
rounds the big house to the garage
apartment, feet black from the path. There
she'll dirty the cool sheets she slips
between without clothes, without a bath,
to replay the night, her pressed and fired
body. Smile, the edge
of a full cup.

Smoothie

In goes the banana.
Three frozen strawberries,
a handful of blues. In goes
grape juice, known for its
dark healing. In goes the Greek
yogurt, thick ivory cream,
protein. In goes green algae.
Honey. In goes the sweet
brilliant gold of a Vermeer
print. In goes the black leather
couch. The TV, the glass
table. Bottles of vodka and
wine. Documentaries and
rom-coms. Dave Brubek
and The Pixies. Why not the
poodle? The king-sized bed?
The blankets and sheets? The
rows of basil beside the house?
In goes windows. In goes grass,
two silver cars. All our cash.
In goes the street, the neighbors.
In goes shingles, the roof. In
goes air, the black sky, planets
and stars. My hand on Don's
shoulder, he looks up. He's got
the Giants on, an important
game, and I hand him a glass,
full to the brim. This is true.
This is the heart. One of us,
someday, will be gone.

Old Joke

There's the joke about the tension that arises
when a man and woman unexpectedly find themselves
alone in a room with a bed. Strangers and friends,

one is pale and kind, belly thick from responding
to emails all day. It's night, and the other's smile's a bit
effusive, body, too wound, feet bound by brown shoes.

He or she is perhaps married to someone they know.

But the primal impulse is a banging
of the funny bone—jerked arm that nearly tips
the glass of water on the bedside table. So close, they can

hear the automatic clock work, so close they are
to laughter, almost dispelling the immediate thought,
the odd-duck pair, upfront duty and way in

the back want. Smiling, she says something about her need
to get back, he laughs, they're moving now to
the door, one and the other on the periphery, how it will go

dark quickly, with a click.

Heat

the end of heat means smoke, ghost, fall, pregnancy—
i tell you, heat the true human religion—undoing ice,
frying meat—we blood-made, of heat ambrosia, cops
packing protection, not yet ghosts cropped from future
films, heat the parole officer's checklist, fire lit under
a glass pipe's bowl—oh hot sauce on hash, on greens,
on eggs, oh cat of the evening who yowls, fecund and
cabbagy—oh hot-air balloon adrift and rainbowed, oh
bucket, oh list, oh blown-clear dream—the mouth's
cinnamon gum, the tongue burned for black coffee,
green tea, steak fries, altogether hungry, the love-
bugs conjoined in a windshield's hot blades, what
vibrating heat, hammers falling on strings, a minuet,
hammers falling on knees, a caveat—for all heat illicit
may we have mercy—kid with her wrist strung in
carlighter burns, red-eye machine with paternity-
news, desperate-head eyes in despair's plastic bag—
from each light a heat, whispering reproach or relief

Heartworks

You're sitting here with me, my closest friend
and only sister, as I attempt to write,
and you (with jet-black needle) try to mend
the pants your son has torn. So we're alike
in where we give our hearts — our own designs —
you to your son, whom you keep snuggled up
with buttons, zippers, snaps (to you entwined),
as though your thread and thimble, bread and cup.
I'm nearly as consumed by my own verse,
needling sonnets, stitching up their rhymes,
as here I must prepare to turn (a curse —
to want a seamless volta for the lines):
But you're a bard, as much as I'm a tailor,
in working past small triumphs, little failures.

China Poem

Public restrooms paperless, a
hole in the ground. Here in
China, she is a foreigner,
literally a squatter. She leans
to assume a forward posture.
But not *too* forward. Careless,
the first day, steaming through
hot Nanjing streets, a head taller
than the men. She is the Great
White Veil, headlights-and-horns
breasts blaring, her eyes behind
movie star shades. In the web
of distressed streets, she is a spy,
more alive here in the struggle
to disengage, engage. She learns
too late sunglasses are unfriendly.
Even the trees, strange. In them,
real magpies. She can't sleep.
How to tweak dollars to yuan?
How to tip? Everything seeming
sleight, taxi drivers circling,
driving up fares. The menu she
can't read, but from which
she must choose. Chicken feet.
Pig kidneys. Fish with bones.
Every part used. How spoiled
is she! How dust-frail and
without grace. If only she knew
how to conjure a storm. On the
arbor outside her window,
wisteria curls, dead petals hang.
She imagines rain, wind, so
many vines stripped clean.

Notes

Section II inspired by Chuck Shepherd's "News of the Weird" columns.

"Dry Spell": italicized portions a quote by Anne Morrow Lindbergh.

Section V inspired by the photographs of Diane Arbus.

TITLES FROM ELIXIR PRESS

Poetry

Circassian Girl by Michelle Mitchell-Foust
Imago Mundi by Michelle Mitchell-Foust
Distance From Birth by Tracy Philpot
Original White Animals by Tracy Philpot
Flow Blue by Sarah Kennedy
A Witch's Dictionary by Sarah Kennedy
The Gold Thread by Sarah Kennedy
Monster Zero by Jay Snodgrass
Drag by Duriel E. Harris
Running the Voodoo Down by Jim McGarrah
Assignation at Vanishing Point by Jane Satterfield
Her Familiars by Jane Satterfield
The Jewish Fake Book by Sima Rabinowitz
Recital by Samn Stockwell
Murder Ballads by Jake Adam York
Floating Girl (Angel of War) by Robert Randolph
Puritan Spectacle by Robert Strong
Keeping the Tigers Behind Us by Glenn J. Freeman
Bonneville by Jenny Mueller
Cities of Flesh and the Dead by Diann Blakely
The Halo Rule by Teresa Leo
Perpetual Care by Katie Cappello
The Raindrop's Gospel: The Trials of St. Jerome and St. Paula by Maurya Simon
Prelude to Air from Water by Sandy Florian
Let Me Open You A Swan by Deborah Bogen
Cargo by Kristin Kelly
Spit by Esther Lee
Rag & Bone by Kathrym Nuernberger
Kingdom of Throat-stuck Luck by George Kalamaras
Mormon Boy by S. Brady Tucker
Nostalgia for the Criminal Past by Kathleen Winter
Little Oblivion by Susan Allspaw
Quelled Communiqués by Chloe Joan Lopez
Stupor by David Ray Vance
Curio by John Nieves
The Rub by Ariana-Sophia Kartsonis
Visiting Indira Gandhi's Palmist by Kirun Kapur
Freaked by Liz Robbins
Looming by Jennifer Franklin
Flammable Matter by Jacob Victorine
Prayer Book for the Anxious by Josephine Yu

Fiction

How Things Break by Kerala Goodkin
Nine Ten Again by Phil Condon
Memory Sickness by Phong Nguyen
Troglodyte by Tracy DeBrincat
The Loss of All Lost Things by Amina Gautier

Limited Edition Chapbooks

Juju by Judy Moffat
Grass by Sean Aden Lovelace
X-testaments by Karen Zealand
Rapture by Sarah Kennedy
Green Ink Wings by Sherre Myers
Orange Reminds You Of Listening by Kristin Abraham
In What I Have Done & What I Have Failed To Do by Joseph P. Wood
Hymn of Ash by George Looney
Bray by Paul Gibbons

FREAKED